William Morris Patterns & Designs

❧❧

by Phoebe Ann Erb

Stemmer House
Publishers

Inquiries should be directed to
Stemmer House Publishers
P.O. Box 89
4 White Brook Road
Gilsum, NH 03448
www.stemmer.com

Printed and bound in the United States of America

First Printing 2002
Second Printing 2009
Third Printing 2011

A Barbara Holdridge book

PHOEBE ANN ERB has been creating print designs for commercial fashion and home furnishings fabrics for the past 26 years. She also teaches textile print design and collects, exhibits and writes about printed handkerchiefs and aprons of the mid-twentieth century. Phoebe is the author of two previous titles in the extensive International Design Library®, listed on the inside back cover: *Floral Designs from Traditional Printed Handkerchiefs* and *Medieval Floral Designs*.

Introduction

"Have nothing in your houses
that you do not know to be useful, or believe to be beautiful."

WILLIAM MORRIS WAS ONE OF THE MOST INFLUENTIAL artist-craftsmen of the nineteenth century. His innovative designs set new standards of taste and have left a lasting mark on the decorative arts.

Morris was born on March 24, 1834 in a countrified suburb at the northeastern edge of London. His father was a businessman who could afford a mansion for his family. The large house sat in a fifty-acre park of orchards and gardens, sheep and cows, pigs and poultry, surrounded by fields of hay and clover along the banks of the Roding River, near Epping Forest. It was "a pretty place, a very jolly place," Morris recalled. Its charm inspired all of Morris's life—in art, in craft, in politics.

As a boy, William wandered the family estate. He loved flowers and studied their forms and colors. He gathered nuts, fished in the river and shot birds and rabbits in the fields. He would ride off on his pony to explore the forest "yard by yard" in search of ancient ruins and medieval churches, making up stories about everything he saw.

Morris attended high school at Marlborough College. Instruction was disorganized, but he took advantage of a library that was filled with books on history and architecture. Always a voracious reader, Morris claimed to have read all of Sir Walter Scott's romantic novels by age seven. He especially loved books about the Middle Ages, which made a deep impression on him. Deciding to take Holy Orders, in 1853 he entered Exeter College, Oxford.

At Oxford, Morris met Edward Burne-Jones, also planning to enter the Church. They both felt isolated from their contemporaries and became friends. Spending hours reading and discussing history, theology and the recently published works of John Ruskin, who greatly influenced their thoughts about art and society, they also wandered the streets of Oxford, which still looked like a medieval town, with its gray stones and wooden sculptures all about. Their visits to cities in France and Belgium fueled their passion for the medieval age. Struck by the contrast with the invasive ugliness of the Industrial Revolution at home, they decided they could improve the world better as artists than as churchmen.

1

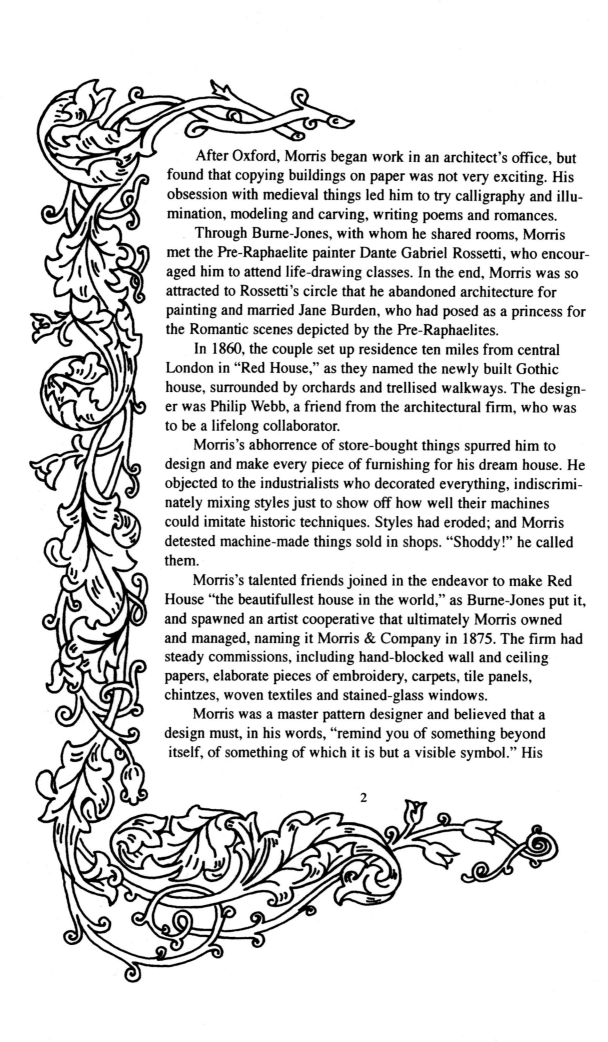

After Oxford, Morris began work in an architect's office, but found that copying buildings on paper was not very exciting. His obsession with medieval things led him to try calligraphy and illumination, modeling and carving, writing poems and romances.

Through Burne-Jones, with whom he shared rooms, Morris met the Pre-Raphaelite painter Dante Gabriel Rossetti, who encouraged him to attend life-drawing classes. In the end, Morris was so attracted to Rossetti's circle that he abandoned architecture for painting and married Jane Burden, who had posed as a princess for the Romantic scenes depicted by the Pre-Raphaelites.

In 1860, the couple set up residence ten miles from central London in "Red House," as they named the newly built Gothic house, surrounded by orchards and trellised walkways. The designer was Philip Webb, a friend from the architectural firm, who was to be a lifelong collaborator.

Morris's abhorrence of store-bought things spurred him to design and make every piece of furnishing for his dream house. He objected to the industrialists who decorated everything, indiscriminately mixing styles just to show off how well their machines could imitate historic techniques. Styles had eroded; and Morris detested machine-made things sold in shops. "Shoddy!" he called them.

Morris's talented friends joined in the endeavor to make Red House "the beautifullest house in the world," as Burne-Jones put it, and spawned an artist cooperative that ultimately Morris owned and managed, naming it Morris & Company in 1875. The firm had steady commissions, including hand-blocked wall and ceiling papers, elaborate pieces of embroidery, carpets, tile panels, chintzes, woven textiles and stained-glass windows.

Morris was a master pattern designer and believed that a design must, in his words, "remind you of something beyond itself, of something of which it is but a visible symbol." His designs evoked the out-of-doors, willows against the sky, branching fruit trees, a tangle of thickets, climbing roses, birds and rabbits. His naturalistic style was revolutionary, bringing lightness into dark Victorian rooms.

With a drawing technique that was always crisp and clean, he constructed patterns on endless variations of diagonal lines or networks of diamonds. He used contrasting large and small forms and secondary patterns to offset the main theme. His use of scrolling leaves, undulating stems and branches in the patterns gave them the impression of spontaneous growth. Birds, animals and human figures, drawn by his co-artists, appear in many of the designs. Morris sometimes adopted the highly stylized forms and mirror-image layouts of early medieval designs. Now and then, he combined a free-flowing style with formalized motifs.

With typical thoroughness, Morris studied old dyeing manuals, experimented with vegetable recipes and set up his own dye works. Greens of every shade, deep indigo and madder red made up his palette, as he aimed to recreate colors in medieval tapestries. He preferred subdued warm secondary or tertiary colors–an antidote to the garishness of the new synthetic dyes used in industry.

Morris never lost his love of old books and undertook the craft of bookmaking. In 1891, he founded Kelmscott Press, "a little typographical adventure," he called it, with the hope of restoring the lost beauty of fifteenth-century craftsmanship. Books of the day were generally ill-designed and ugly. He designed new typefaces and had paper made to his own specifications. Some monumental projects were taken on, including the complete works of Geoffrey Chaucer. Kelmscott books are filled with wood-engraved pictures–idealized balletic figures in mythical landscapes–by Edward Burne-Jones, Walter Crane and others.

The decorated initials, borders and frames drawn by Morris illustrate his deep love of meandering, intertwining plant forms.

3

During the 1880s, political activity dominated Morris's attention. "I have only one subject to lecture on," Morris proclaimed, "the relation of art to labor." In all of his speeches and writings, Morris discussed art in terms of its meaning in everyday life and its contribution to happiness. He felt that the only happy condition for the worker was to unite art and craft, as they had been in medieval times. The division of labor in factories robbed the worker of any creativity and joy in work; and to him this was immoral. He railed against the industrialists who put profit above quality. "I do not want art for a few," he declared, "any more than education for a few, or freedom for a few."

His critics called him hypocritical. Here was a wealthy artist whose prosperous business supplied goods to the rich, while he harangued about the incompatibility of art and capitalism. But to him, the fact that his high standards placed his goods beyond the reach of many was an indictment of the current commercialism. It made him angry, but he would not lower his standards. He may have failed to bridge the gulf between art and industry in his own day, but it is difficult to overstate Morris's influence on subsequent generations in raising the standards of design for all levels of society.

William Morris died in 1896, "having done more than ten men," as his doctor remarked. Over a century later, his wallpapers and textiles are still in production, by hand as well as by machine, and are no longer limited to the few. One wonders what he would think of the giftwraps, notebooks, bookmarks and a host of other products adorned with his designs and available to all.

P .A. E.

Selected Reading List

William Morris has been both author and subject of many books and articles, and is cited countless times by authors writing about art, design, literature and Socialism. Full-color reproductions of his patterns and designs can be seen in some of the following titles:

Baker, Derek W. *The Flowers of William Morris*. Chicago: Chicago ReviewPress,1996

Mackail, J. W. *The Life of William Morris*. New York: Dover, 1995

MacCarthy, Fiona. *William Morris: A Life for Our Time*. New York: Knopf, 1995

Morris, William. *The Collected Works of William Morris*. Edited by May Morris. 24 volumes. New York: Russell and Russell, 1966

———. *The Ideal Book*. Berkeley: University of California Press, 1982

——— . *Selected Writings and Designs*. Edited by Asa Briggs. New York: Penguin Books, 1962

———.*William Morris by Himself*. Edited by Gillian Naylor. Boston: Little, Brown, 1988

Parry, Linda.*William Morris Textiles*. Avenell, NJ: Crescent Books, 1995

Sewter, A.C. *The Stained Glass of William Morris and His Circle*. New Haven: Yale University Press, 1975.

Plate Descriptions

The drawings on the following pages are details taken from the textiles, books, tiles and stained-glass windows designed and produced by William Morris and others involved in Morris & Company and the Kelmscott Press. Most of the motifs have been reduced or enlarged for the purposes of this book. Identification includes the name and approximate date of each design, as well as any contributions of other artists.

Front cover: Bird, woven wool, 1878
Back cover: Golden Bough, woven silk and linen, 1888
Title page: Rose and Lily, woven silk and wool, 1893
Plates 1-40

1. Flower pot. Embroidered cushion cover, 1880
2. Birds and Anemone. Chintz and wallpaper, 1881-1882
3. Birds and Anemone. Chintz and wallpaper, 1881-1882
4. Compton. Chintz and wallpaper, 1896
5. Left: Corncockle. Printed linen, 1883
   Right: Daffodil. Chintz, 1891
6. Top: Flowerpots. Printed cotton, 1883
   Lower left: Tile, designed by Kate Faulkner or John Henry Dearle, 1875-1880
   Lower right: The Artichoke embroidered panel, 1877
7. Left: Wood Beyond the World. Designed by Edward Burne-Jones, 1894
   Top right: Small Barr Hammersmith carpet, c.1880
   Lower right: The Story of the Glittering Plain, 1894
8. Left: Minstrel, floral detail, stained glass, 1874
   Right: Kennet. Printed and woven textiles, 1883
9. Top left: Geoffrey Chaucer tile. Designed by Edward Burne-Jones, 1863
   Top right and bottom: Brother Rabbit. Printed cotton, 1882
10. Left: The Water of Wondrous Isles, 1879
    Right: embroidery design, 1875
11. Left: Corncockle. Chintz, 1883
    Right: Birds. Woven wool, 1878
12. Top left: The Story of the Glittering Plain, 1894
    Top right: Swan tile, 1862-1865
    Lower: Peacock and Dragon, woven wool, 1878
13. The Wood Beyond the World, 1894
14. Redcar carpet, 1881-1885
15. Left: Woodpecker tapestry, c. 1885
    Right: Love Is Enough, 1871
16. Top: Strawberry Thief. Printed cotton, 1883
    Lower left: Sunflower tile, 1870
    Lower right: Primrose tile, 1882-1885
17. Top left: Tulip trellis tile, 1870
    Top right: Powdered wallpaper, 1874
    Center right: Longden tile, c. 1870. Probably designed by Philip Webb
    Lower left: Powdered wallpaper, 1874
    Lower right: Strawberry Thief. Printed cotton, 1883
18. Left: Minstrel tile, c. 1872
    Right: The Orchard or The Seasons Tapestry, 1890. Figure designed by Edward Burne-Jones
19. Left: The Orchard or The Seasons Tapestry, 1890
    Right: Minstrel tile, c. 1872. Figure designed by Edward Burne-Jones
20. Left: Oxford Union ceiling, 1874-15
    Top and lower right: Rose chintz 1883
21. Top: Evenlode chintz, 1883
    Top and center left: St. James woven silk damask, 1881
    Lower left: Lodden printed cotton, 1884
    Center and lower right: Daisy tiles, 1862

Plate Descriptions, Continued

22. Left: Ceiling design, 1880
    Right: Little Flowers Hammersmith carpet, c.1890
23. Wey Chintz, 1883
24. Dove and Rose woven textile, 1879
25. Medway chintz, 1885
26. Top left: Cherwell printed velvet, 1880
    Center left: Golden Bough woven silk and wool, 1888
    Lower left: Hand-knotted rug, late 19th century
    Right: Bird and Palm Tree, date unknown
27. Top, center left and lower right.: Stained glass by Philip Webb, 1859-1860
    Lower left: Fruit or Pomegranate wallpaper, 1864
    Right: Willow and vine for wallpaper, never produced, undated
28. Left: Larkspur wallpaper and printed cotton, 1872
    Right: Daffodil chintz, 1891
29. Top: Tulip and willow printed textile, 1873
    Bottom: Buller's Wood Hammersmith carpet, c. 1880
30. Bachelor's Button wallpaper, 1892
31. Willow Bough wallpaper, 1887
32. Wild Tulip wallpaper, 1884
33. Top and center left: Carpet motifs, c. 1880
    Top right: Rose and Lily woven silk and wool, 1893
    Bottom: Golden Bough woven silk and linen, 1888
34. Top left: Scroll tile 1870
    Right: Cross Twigs woven textile by John Henry Deale, 1898
    Lower left: Ceiling decoration, 1880-1881
35. Top: Grafton wallpaper, 1883
    Lower left: The Artichoke embroidered panel, 1877
    Lower right: Hammersmith carpet, 1890
36. Tulip, printed cotton, 1875
37. Ceiling paper, 1881
38. Angel of the Annunciation, stained glass, 1862
39. Virgin of the Annunciation, stained glass, 1862
40 Trellis wallpaper, birds designed by Philip Webb, 1862

Below: Black-thorn wallpaper, 1892

Dedication

For Kimball & Gillian

7

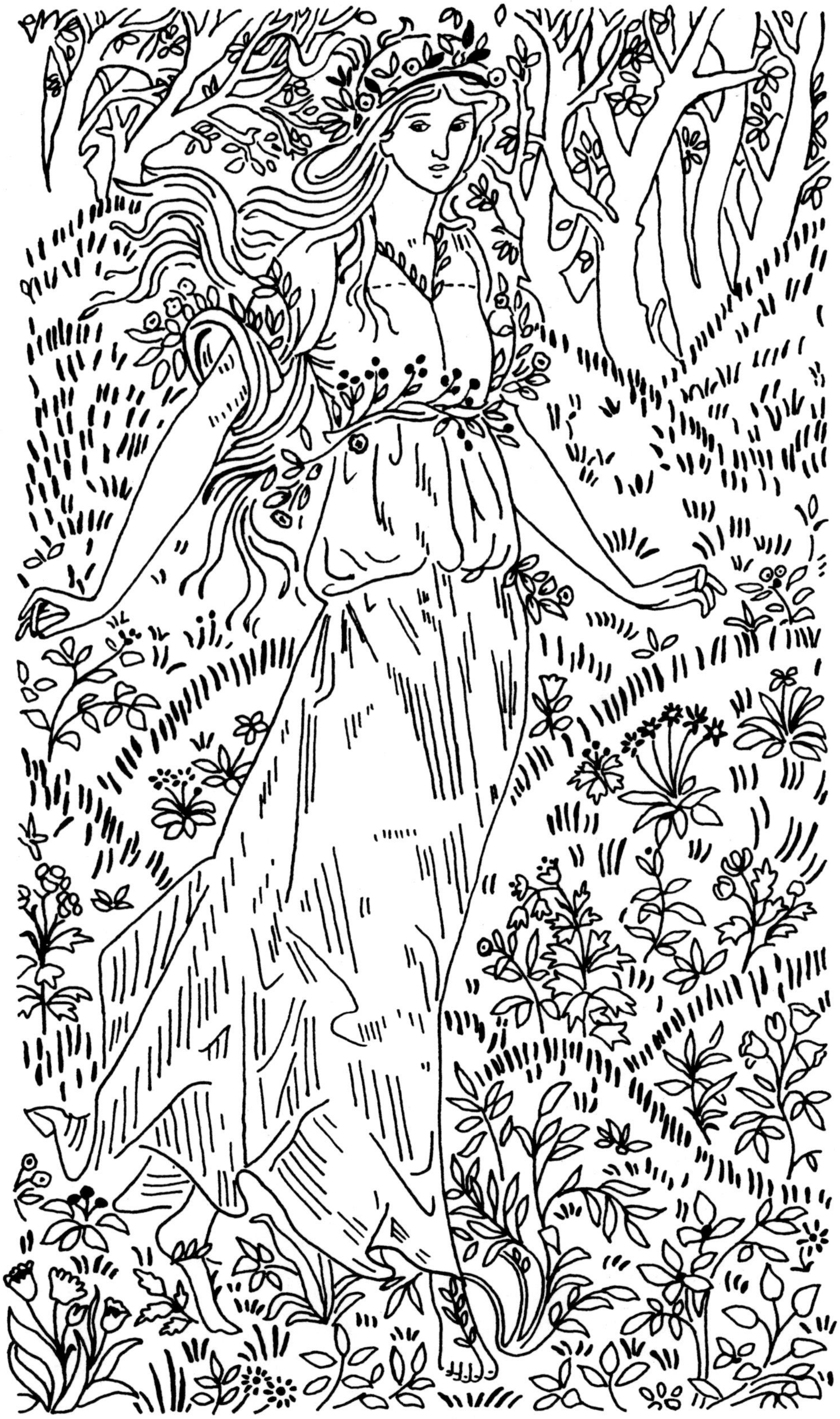

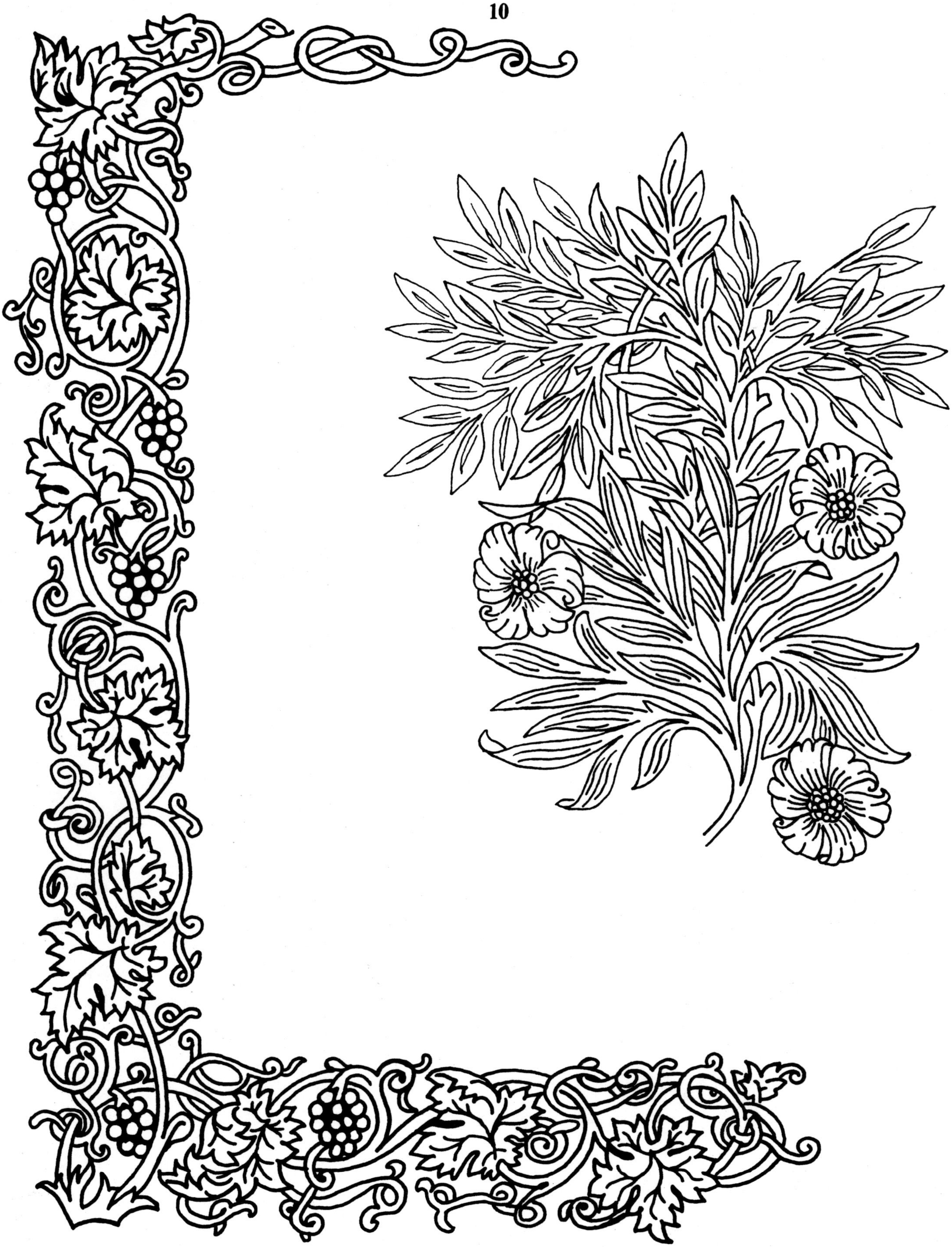

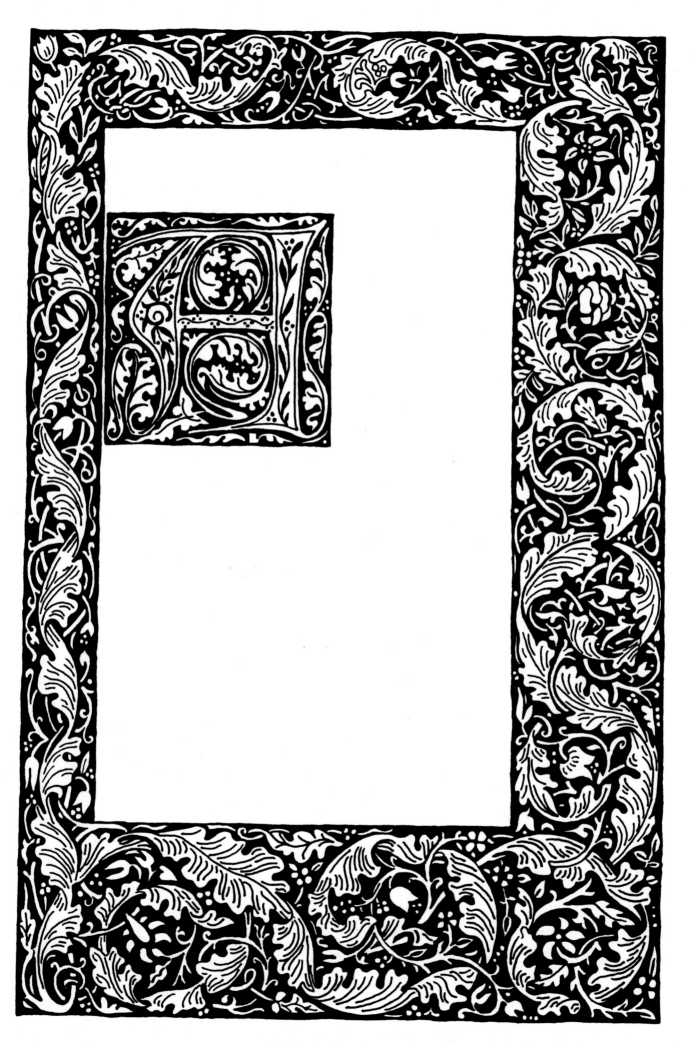

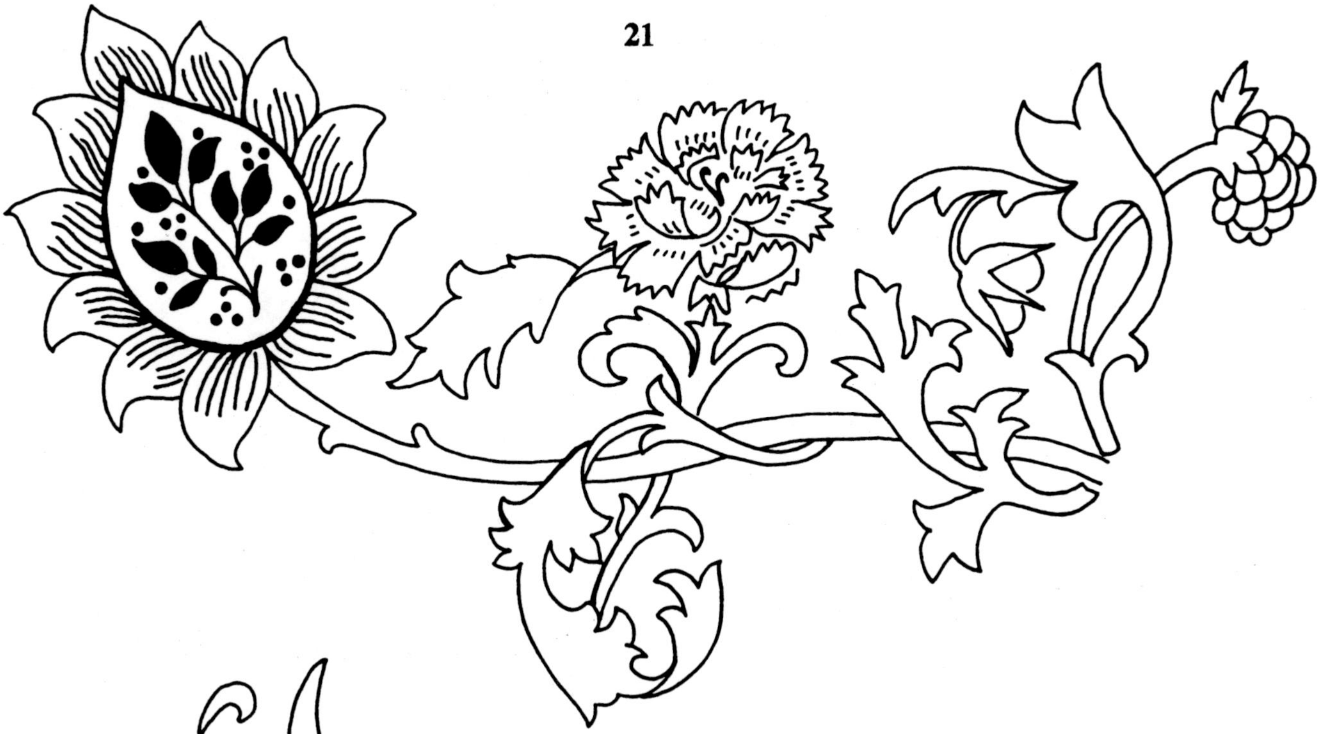

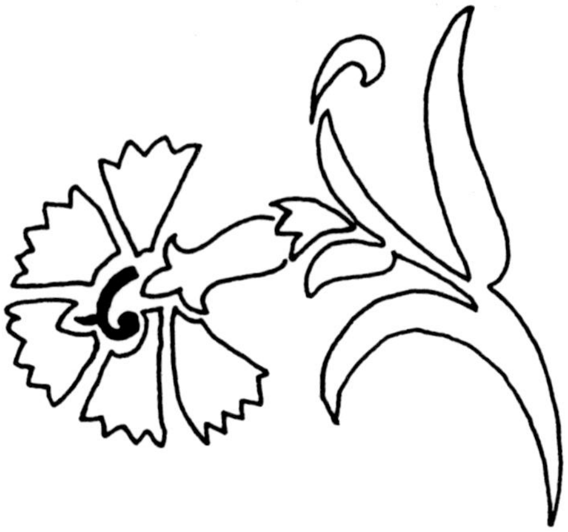

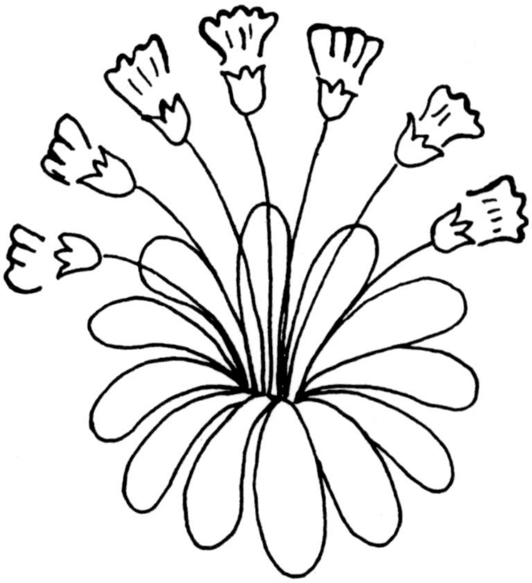

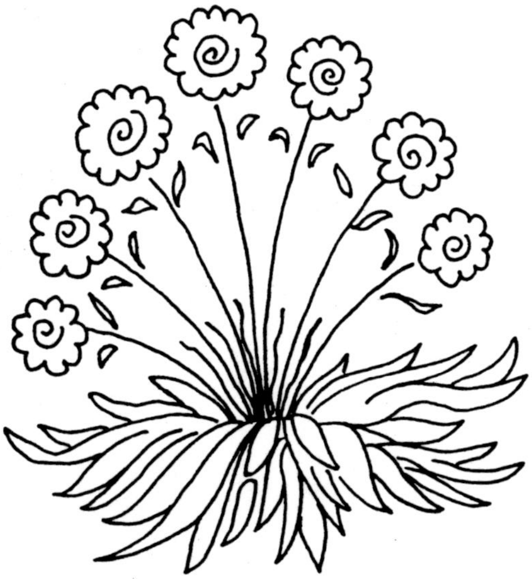